LADY PENELOPE'S
COCKTAILS

50 SPLENDID
COCKTAIL RECIPES
by Sarah Tomley

CASSELL
ILLUSTRATED

An Hachette UK Company
www.hachette.co.uk

First published in Great Britain in 2015 by
Cassell, a division of Octopus Publishing Group Ltd
Carmelite House
50 Victoria Embankment
London EC4Y 0DZ
www.octopusbooks.co.uk

Recipes in this book have previously appeared in other books published by Hamlyn.

ISBN 9781844038282

A CIP catalogue record for this book is available from the British Library

Printed and bound in China

10 9 8 7 6 5 4 3 2 1

Measurements note
The measure that has been used in the recipes is based on a bar jigger, which is 25 ml (1 fl oz).
If preferred, a different volume can be used, providing the proportions are kept constant
within a drink and suitable adjustments are made to spoon measurements, where they occur.
Standard level spoon measurements are used throughout: 1 tablespoon = one 15 ml spoon;
1 teaspoon = one 5 ml spoon.

Safety note
Drinking excessive alcohol can significantly damage your health. The UK Department of Health
recommends that men do not exceed 21 units of alcohol per week (no more than 4 per day),
and women 14 units per week (no more than 3 per day). Never operate a vehicle when you
have been drinking alcohol. Octopus Publishing Group accepts no liability or responsibility for
any consequences resulting from the use of or reliance upon the information contained herein.

CONTENTS

INTRODUCTION

Anyone who truly appreciates the seriousness of life and the lurking possibility of death around every corner also, undoubtedly, appreciates the importance of frivolity. And what could be more frivolous than the cocktail? A cheeky little thing with a deceptive punch that can knock some much-needed life into you on the dullest of days and calm you down in times of high pressure, when the nerves, quite frankly, jangle most unattractively.

And there you have it; not only a wonderful nerve tonic, but also a jolly good accessory. I sometimes choose a cocktail by colour to go with my outfit – usually to blend in, but occasionally in complementary hues – but then I am a stickler for detail. It's what makes my work with International Rescue so valuable. I never miss a thing, and

I can catch the whiff of a Cuban cigar from several miles away with the wind in the right direction. This rather keen scenting ability can prove less than fortuitous on occasion, especially when one has been trapped on a yacht with a less-than-salubrious kidnapper for some time, as I found to my cost with that dreadful man named Carl. Still, at least he had the decency to allow me to 'fix my face' and thereby use my face-powder-compact radio. Men! They're so easily distracted by feminine charms, which I find terribly handy when combatting international villains.

But I digress. This book is dedicated to my favourite cocktail maker – Parker – who manages to move seamlessly from cracking good driver to bodyguard and then to butler in a flash. Where would I be without him? Probably still in that dreadful basement with Sir Jeremy Hodge – gas everywhere and no escape in sight. Now there's a story.

SIMPLY SPLENDID CLASSICS

A cocktail party is a delightful way of liquidating social obligations to any number of people all at once. A cocktail on one's own, or à deux, on the other hand, is one of life's delights, especially after a day of perilous excitement. Whatever the occasion, these little classics can always be counted on to fit the bill.

COSMOPOLITAN

MAKES: I

6 ice cubes, cracked
I measure vodka
½ measure Cointreau
I measure cranberry
 juice

juice of ½ lime
orange rind twist,
 to decorate

Put the cracked ice into a cocktail shaker.
Add all the remaining ingredients and shake
until a frost forms on the outside of the shaker.
This can become inelegant and is best avoided
in company – luckily I have Parker always on
hand for these crucial little jobs.

Strain the pretty drink into a chilled Martini
glass. Decorate with an orange rind twist for
perfection, and enjoy.

"Who doesn't love a Cosmo? It can absolutely be counted upon to lift the spirits and make the tiresome exploits of ill-intentioned men simply drift away."

"I do love Pernod, and this classic cocktail has the added frisson of the wonderful Angostura bitters. Peychaud's Bitters, which were used in the original whisky Sazerac, are equally splendid."

VODKA SAZERAC

MAKES: 1

1 sugar cube
2 drops Angostura
  bitters
3 drops Pernod

3–4 ice cubes
2 measures vodka
lemonade, to top up

Put a sugar cube into an old-fashioned glass and shake the bitters onto it. Add the Pernod and swirl it around to coat the inside of the glass. Drop in the ice cubes and pour in the vodka, already chilled if possible. Top up with lemonade and stir gently. Ready when you are!

MOSCOW MULE

"Vodka and ginger beer give this cocktail a divine little kick that's the perfect pick-me-up after a particularly trying mission."

MAKES: 1

6–8 ice cubes, cracked
2 measures vodka
juice of 2 limes
ginger beer, to top up

lime slice, to decorate
spiral of lime rind,
  to decorate

Put the cracked ice into a highball glass. Add the vodka and lime juice, stir and top with ginger beer. Decorate with a lime slice and a lime rind spiral if time allows – otherwise drink unadorned. Delicious.

BLOODY MARY

"How I wish I had known the legendary 'Pete' Petiot, who worked at the famous Harry's New York Bar in Paris after World War 1. He invented this fabulous drink and was obviously a complete whizz at everything he did."

MAKES: 1

4–5 ice cubes
2 measures vodka
1 dash lemon juice
Worcestershire sauce, to taste

tomato juice, to top up
½ teaspoon cayenne pepper
salt and pepper
celery sticks, to decorate

Put some ice cubes into a highball glass. Pour over the vodka and lemon juice, add Worcestershire sauce to taste and top up with tomato juice. Add the cayenne pepper and season to taste with salt and pepper. Remember that some like it hot! Stir to allow the ice to add a contrasting chill, then decorate with celery stalks (if you have some to hand) and drink without further ado.

CLASSIC DRY MARTINI

"An ex-boyfriend from my finishing-school days used to say that this version is called a Naked Martini, but I can't help feeling he was trying overly hard to make himself memorable. His name quite escapes me now."

MAKES: 1

½ measure dry
   vermouth
1 measure frozen gin

1 green olive or lemon
   twist, to decorate

Swirl the vermouth around the inside of a chilled martini glass, then discard the excess. Pour in the frozen gin and add an olive or lemon twist. Simple, elegant and unfussy – naked or not.

SINGAPORE SLING

"Ah, Singapore — so romantic and yet so fantastically forward-thinking. Jeff Tracy and I have bought some wondrous gadgets here, while staying at Raffles Hotel, where this little number was created by Ngiam Tong Boon. He was said to be a complete darling."

MAKES: 1
ice cubes
1 measure gin
½ measure cherry brandy
¼ measure Cointreau
¼ measure Bénédictine
½ measure grenadine
½ measure fresh lime juice
5 measures pineapple juice
1 dash Angostura bitters
pineapple slice and cocktail cherry,
    to decorate

Put some ice cubes with all the other ingredients into a cocktail shaker and shake well. Don't overdo it. Strain over ice cubes in a tall glass, decorate with a pineapple slice and a cherry or anything else pretty and edible that comes to hand.

TOM COLLINS

MAKES: 2

4 measures gin
½ measure lemon juice
2 teaspoons sugar
  syrup

ice cubes
soda water, to top up
lemon slices, to
  decorate

Divide the gin, lemon juice, and sugar syrup between 2 highball glasses. Stir well and fill the glasses with ice cubes. Top up with soda water and add a lemon slice to each glass. This is perfect on a hot and rather trying day.

"*Mr Tom Collins was the kind of nefarious character that one comes across only too often when working with International Rescue. However, his drink is very fine indeed.*"

GIMLET

"My father, Sir Hugh Creighton-Ward, was very fond of a quick gimlet before dinner. On occasion, he was even known to mix it himself, and he was a stickler for protocol!"

MAKES: 1

2 measures gin
1 measure lime cordial
ice cubes
½ measure water
lime wedge, to decorate

Put the gin and lime cordial into a mixing glass (Parker often leaves these on the drinks tray) then fill it up with ice cubes and stir well. Strain into a chilled martini glass, add the water, and squeeze the lime into the drink before popping in the wedge too (unless you are terribly strong and have squeezed it beyond recognition).

PIMM'S CUP COCKTAIL

MAKES: 2

ice cubes
2 measures Pimm's
    No. I Cup
2 measures gin
4 measures lemonade

4 measures ginger ale
cucumber, apple and
    orange slices, and
    a few mint leaves,
    to decorate

Fill 2 highball glasses with ice cubes. Add the remaining ingredients, one by one in order, over the ice. Put in plenty of cucumber and fruit slices, poke in a few mint leaves and serve. Fantastically fruity and refreshing.

"Ah, Pimm's. Englishness distilled. Of course one can only drink this in summer, but perhaps its rarity makes it all the finer when one finally gets one's hands on it. This is an absolute must for a garden party."

DAIQUIRI FROZEN MANGO

MAKES: I

crushed ice
½ mango, peeled and
   stoned
I measure fresh lime
   juice

2 measures white rum
I teaspoon icing sugar
mango slices, to
   decorate

Put a small scoop of crushed ice into a food processor or blender. Add the mango, lime juice, rum and icing sugar, then blend until smooth. Serve in a small glass and decorate with mango slices, if you have time. If you are drinking it en route to deal with desperate men, the quicker the better.

"This is simply the only drink to have before a fast and ferocious mission. It does the trick instantly and makes one feel braver by the minute. The mango is purely optional – don't for a moment feel in any way obliged."

MOJITO

MAKES: 2

16 mint leaves, plus
    sprigs to decorate
1 lime, cut into wedges
4 teaspoons granulated
    sugar
crushed ice
4 measures white rum
soda water, to top up

*Divide the mint leaves, lime, and sugar between
2 highball glasses and muddle the ingredients
a little. Fill the glasses to the top with crushed
ice, then add the rum, stir, and top up with soda
water. Decorate with mint sprigs and serve.
Minty mojito heaven.*

"*This delightful cocktail takes its name from the word 'mojo', which means 'to place a little spell'. It certainly places a spell on me, and Parker has been known to be markedly less attentive after drinking one.*"

RUM OLD-FASHIONED

"Call me old-fashioned, but I love this classic little drink. It certainly packs a punch and it was a favourite of one of my old spymasters. (To tell you more would be to tempt fate and disaster.)"

MAKES: 1

3 ice cubes
1 dash Angostura
   bitters
1 dash lime bitters
½ teaspoon sugar
½ measure water

2 measures white rum
½ measure dark rum
lime wedge, to
   decorate

Stir 1 ice cube with the bitters, sugar and water in a heavy-based old-fashioned glass until the sugar has dissolved. Add the white rum, stir, and add the remaining ice cubes. Add the dark rum and stir once again. Decorate with a lime wedge. Drink leisurely and only with friends.

CAIPIRINHA

"I was first offered a caipirinha by Jeff Tracy on one very hot afternoon at Tracy Island, shortly after helping MI5 agent Bondson recover stolen plans for a nuclear weapon. We certainly needed a drink and this was just the ticket."

MAKES: 1

6 lime wedges
2 teaspoons brown sugar
2 measures cachaça
4–5 ice cubes, crushed

Place 3 of the lime wedges in a large tumbler or old-fashioned glass and add the brown sugar and cachaça. Mix well, mashing the limes slightly to make a little juice. Top up with the crushed ice cubes, and decorate with the remaining lime wedges.

MINT JULEP

MAKES: 1

9 young mint sprigs,
plus extra to
decorate

1 teaspoon sugar syrup
crushed ice
3 measures bourbon

Muddle the mint and sugar syrup in a highball glass. Fill the glass with crushed ice, pour the bourbon over the ice and stir gently. Pack in more crushed ice and stir until a frost forms. Wrap the glass in a table napkin, unless you are feeling extraordinarily nonplussed, and serve decorated with a mint sprig.

"Sir Jeremy Hodge, who was good enough to put lots of money behind International Rescue in its early days, was very fond of a whisky and soda. When feeling indulgent and in company, he could sometimes be persuaded to join me in a mint julep."

PARISIAN

PARISIAN

MAKES: 1

crushed ice
1 measure brandy
½ measure Calvados
1 measure fresh
   lemon juice

sugar syrup, to taste
½ measure Poire
   William
berries and mint leaves,
   to decorate

*Fill a glass with crushed ice. Add the brandy,
Calvados, lemon juice and sugar syrup to
taste. Pour the Poire William over the top and
decorate with berries and mint leaves. Santé!*

*"I always say that in Paris, one should
drink Pernod. However, Parisian friends
from Roedean, my erstwhile boarding
school, insisted on drinking Calvados.
Matron was not best pleased."*

MARGARITA

"This is a cocktail-party favourite, because one can leave jugs liberally distributed around the room for guests to serve themselves, should waiting staff be hard to find."

MAKES: I

1 lime wedge
rock salt
ice cubes
2 measures tequila

I measure fresh lime juice
I measure triple sec
lime wheel, to decorate

Moisten the rim of a margarita glass with the lime wedge and frost with the salt. Half-fill a cocktail shaker with ice cubes. Add all the remaining ingredients and shake until a frost forms on the outside of the shaker. Try to maintain composure if forced to do this oneself. Strain into the glass and decorate with a lime wheel. If entertaining guests, simply ask one of your staff to make up a jug of margarita using these proportions. It's terribly easy.

BELLINI

"Champagne is the perfect celebratory drink after a successful mission, and a Bellini is a terrific way to chalk up yet another victory for our wonderful team. Villains really pose no threat to the world as long as Thunderbirds are Go!"

MAKES: 2
4 measures peach juice
8 measures chilled champagne
2 dashes grenadine (optional)
peach wedges, to decorate

Mix together the peach juice and chilled champagne in a large mixing glass. Add the grenadine (if it takes your fancy). Pour the mixed drink into 2 champagne flutes, decorate each glass with a peach wedge and hand the second drink to your guest. The bliss of this cocktail is that it still leaves you with around half a bottle of champagne to drink over dinner. Time allowing, of course.

ISLAND HIGHBALLS

Tracy Island tends to be hot — terribly hot, on occasion, when the boys are experimenting with new toys — and at cocktail hour a highball refreshes the spirit. I sometimes visit this South Pacific paradise en route to my farm in Bonga Bonga, Australia, and always aim for cocktail hour.

TRACY ISLAND FRAGRANCE

TRACY ISLAND FRAGRANCE

"Some people know this cocktail as Green Island Fragrance, because it hails from the gorgeous island of Mauritius, but it will always be connected to Tracy Island for me."

MAKES: 2

3 measures vodka

1 measure Midori

2 measures lemon juice

2 measures pineapple juice

2 dashes sugar syrup

ice cubes, plus crushed ice to serve

2 lemon wedges

Put the vodka, Midori, lemon juice and pineapple juice into a cocktail shaker and add the sugar syrup and some ice cubes. Put some crushed ice into 2 highball glasses. Shake and strain into the glasses. Squeeze a lemon wedge over each drink, then drop it into the glass, and serve with straws to add to that holiday feeling.

SEA BREEZE

"The grapefruit gives this long, cool drink a tinge of bitterness that is perfect for sharpening the senses but cooling the nerves before a tricky mission."

MAKES: 2

ice cubes
2 measures vodka
4 measures cranberry juice

2 measures grapefruit juice
lime wedges, to decorate

Fill 2 highball glasses with ice cubes, pour over the vodka, cranberry juice and grapefruit juice and stir well. Decorate with lime wedges and serve with some sharp lime wedges on the side, for those who need a little extra zing.

LE MANS

"I do love a fast car, and Le Mans is simply full of them during the famous race in June every year. This drink is a toast to fearless drivers everywhere, including my own dear Parker."

MAKES: 1
2–3 ice cubes, cracked
1 measure Cointreau
½ measure vodka
soda water, to top up
lemon slice, to decorate

Put the ice into a Collins glass. Add the Cointreau and vodka, stir, then top up with soda water. Float the lemon slice on top and serve.

TRACY ISLAND ICED TEA

"This is a rather cheeky, new-generation cocktail. Jeff Tracy scorns it in favour of something more traditional, but it is a keen favourite with his boys, who seem quite unbothered by the extraordinary alcoholic mix."

MAKES: 2

1 measure vodka
1 measure gin
1 measure white rum
1 measure tequila
lots of ice cubes

1 measure Cointreau
1 measure lemon juice
cola, to top up
lemon slices, to decorate

Put the vodka, gin, rum, tequila, Cointreau and lemon juice in a cocktail shaker with some ice cubes and shake to mix. Strain into 2 highball glasses filled with ice cubes and top up with cola. Decorate with lemon slices and serve with caution.

ISLAND HIGHBALLS

GINGER RICKY

"If one is offered a pineapple cocktail while reclining near actual pineapples, it is utterly irresistible. Failing that, a waiter wearing a pineapple-adorned apron will often pass muster as a reasonable excuse."

MAKES: 1

4 x 1-inch (2.5-cm) cubes
   pineapple
1½ measures London dry gin
½ measure ginger juice

1 teaspoon lime juice
ice cubes
3½ measures dry ginger ale
pineapple leaf, to decorate

Muddle the pineapple in a cocktail shaker, then add the gin and the ginger and lime juices. Shake well, strain, and pour into a Collins glass filled with ice cubes. Top up with the ginger ale and decorate with a pineapple leaf.

(I sometimes like to make this cocktail with ginger juice, which can be obtained by blitzing some fresh ginger in a blender or something similarly ferocious.)

TANQSTREAM

"I can't help thinking that this cocktail sounds rather like one of the Thunderbird fleet, and it very often proves to be equally effective at cheering one's spirits."

MAKES: 2

cracked ice cubes
4 measures Tanqueray
   gin
1 measure lime juice
6 measures soda or
   tonic water

1 measure crème
   de cassis
lime slices and
   mixed berries,
   to decorate

Put some cracked ice with the gin and lime juice into a cocktail shaker and shake to mix. Strain into 2 highball glasses, each half-filled with cracked ice. For a dry Tanqstream, add soda water; for a less dry drink, add tonic water. Stir in the crème de cassis, and decorate with the lime slices and mixed berries.

PINEAPPLE MOJITO

PINEAPPLE MOJITO

"Of course any kind of mojito is divine, but the citrus kick to this mojito guarantees that it's in a class of its own. Rather like myself."

MAKES: 1

6 mint leaves
4 pineapple chunks
2 teaspoons soft brown
  sugar
2 measures golden
  rum

crushed ice
pineapple juice, to
  top up
pineapple wedge
  and mint sprig,
  to decorate

Muddle the mint leaves, pineapple chunks and sugar in a cocktail shaker. Add the rum and shake well. Strain into a glass filled with crushed ice, top up with pineapple juice and stir. Decorate with a pineapple wedge and a mint sprig. Sip decorously.

PINK RUM

MAKES: 1

3 drops Angostura bitters
3–4 ice cubes
2 measures white rum
2 measures cranberry juice
1 measure soda water
lime slice, to decorate

Shake the bitters into a highball glass and swirl it around. (If you are claiming to be on a rigorous detox regime, try using a rocks glass as shown here – it transforms the cocktail into a vision of innocence.) Add the ice cubes, then pour in the rum, cranberry juice, and soda water. Decorate with a lime slice. Terribly simple, divinely delicious.

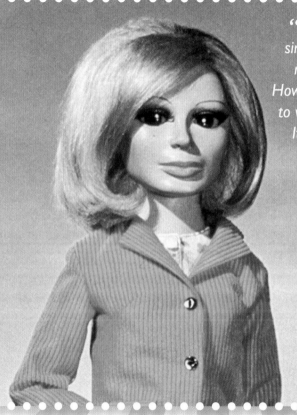

"Pink drinks make my heart sing — mainly because they go rather well with my outfits. However, please don't feel obliged to wear pink while drinking this. It goes perfectly well with a complementary green."

"*Virgil and Gordon once pretended to have found a lobster on the south beach of Tracy Island, and I was so bewitched by the idea that I believed them. This cocktail was concocted in honour of that regrettable experience.*"

LOBSTER ON SOUTH BEACH

LOBSTER ON SOUTH BEACH

MAKES: 2

2 measures white rum
2 measures coconut rum
2 measures mango purée
4 measures mandarin juice
(fresh, if possible)

2 measures coconut cream
8 pineapple chunks
crushed ice
pineapple leaves and mango
slices, to decorate

Put the white and coconut rums, mango purée, mandarin juice, coconut cream and pineapple chunks into a food processor with some crushed ice and blend. Transfer to 2 large highball glasses, decorate with pineapple leaves and mango slices (perched perilously on the side of the glass) and serve.

One can make a Piña Colada quite easily too, using virtually the same mix. Put 2 measures of white rum, 4 measures of coconut cream and 4 measures of pineapple juice in a cocktail shaker. Shake, strain, decorate and serve. An excellent alternative.

MONTE CARLO SLING

"*I had such fun masquerading as the model Gail Williams on my yacht when it was anchored off Monte Carlo one summer. Despite a ticking bomb and threat to my life, I insisted on fixing my make-up. And then Parker lost my yacht while gambling! What a day.*"

MAKES: 2

10 seedless grapes, plus extra
   to decorate
crushed ice
2 measures brandy
1 measure peach liqueur

2 measures ruby port
2 measures lemon juice
1 measure orange juice
2 dashes orange bitters
4 measures champagne

Muddle 5 grapes in the base of each highball glass, then fill the glass with crushed ice. Put all the other ingredients, except the champagne, into a cocktail shaker and add more ice. Shake well and strain into the glasses. Top up with the champagne, decorate with grapes and serve. Oddly bobbly, but distinctly palatable.

ST LUCIA OR BUST

"Every now and then one comes across people gambling whole islands, putting even the Duchess and her gambling habits in the shade. I imagine this is the perfect drink while acting so flamboyantly."

MAKES: 1

4–5 ice cubes
1 measure Curaçao
1 measure dry
   vermouth
juice of ½ orange

1 teaspoon grenadine
2 measures white rum
orange rind spiral and
   cocktail cherry, to
   decorate

Put the ice cubes into a cocktail shaker and pour over the Curaçao, vermouth, orange juice, grenadine and rum. Shake until a frost forms, then pour into a highball glass. Decorate with an orange spiral and a cherry, if you must.

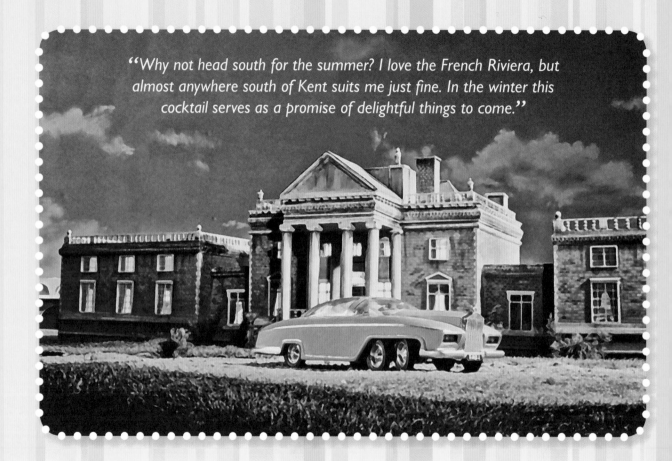

"Why not head south for the summer? I love the French Riviera, but almost anywhere south of Kent suits me just fine. In the winter this cocktail serves as a promise of delightful things to come."

SOUTH FOR THE SUMMER

SOUTH FOR THE SUMMER

MAKES: 2

4 teaspoons grenadine
4 measures tequila
6 measures orange
   juice
8 pineapple chunks

crushed ice
pineapple leaves,
   to decorate
orange rind spirals,
   to decorate

Pour half the grenadine into each glass. Put the tequila, orange juice and pineapple chunks (fresh, please!) into a blender with some crushed ice and blend until it resembles melting snow. Pour the mixture over the grenadine. Decorate each glass with a pineapple leaf and an orange rind spiral and stir just before serving. A southern delight.

BAJA SOUR

"The sour taste here is provided by the orange bitters, but it reminds me of the sour faces of those desperate men so easily thwarted by our fabulous International Rescue team. Will they never learn?"

MAKES: 2

ice cubes
2½ measures tequila
4 teaspoons sugar
  syrup
2½ measures lemon
  juice

4 dashes orange bitters
1 egg white
2 tablespoons
  Amontillado sherry
lemon or lime wedges,
  to decorate

Put 8–10 ice cubes into a cocktail shaker with the tequila, sugar syrup, lemon juice, bitters and egg white then shake vigorously (the drink, silly!). Pour into 2 highball glasses and drizzle over the sherry. Decorate each glass with lemon or lime wedges and do not wince while drinking.

MANSION FAVOURITES

The first Lord Creighton-Ward built the family mansion in the days of Queen Elizabeth I. Unfortunately he was careless enough to burn it down, but the family rebuilt it with all mod cons in 1730, and I have added a few touches myself. Parker is surprisingly good with the radio and alarm systems – one might almost suppose he had a criminal past…

"If one has been up all night, Chambord is just the thing. A rich but delicate liqueur, it is made from red and black raspberries, honey, vanilla, citrus peel and Cognac. Certainly not to be wasted on the unworthy."

SWALLOW DIVE BEFORE DAWN

SWALLOW DIVE BEFORE DAWN

MAKES: 1

ice cubes, plus crushed
    ice to serve
1 measure honey vodka
1 measure Chambord

1 measure lime juice
4 raspberries, plus
    2 to decorate

*Put some ice cubes and all the other ingredients
into a cocktail shaker. Shake well. Put some
crushed ice in a rocks glass and pour in the
cocktail. Top up with more crushed ice and
decorate with the 2 extra raspberries. This is
absolutely one to make for oneself. Secretly
and with guilty pleasure.*

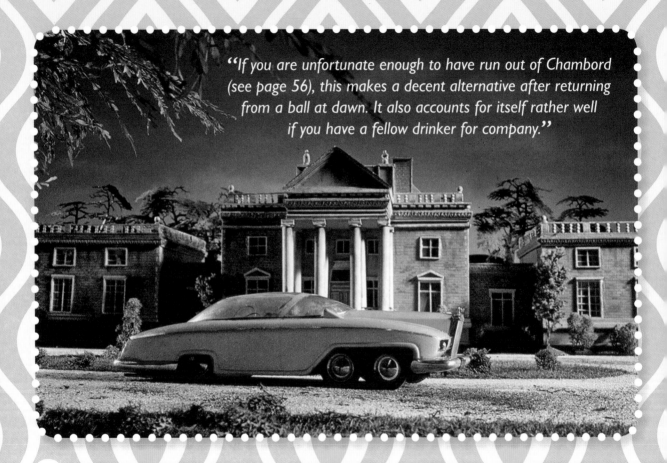

"*If you are unfortunate enough to have run out of Chambord (see page 56), this makes a decent alternative after returning from a ball at dawn. It also accounts for itself rather well if you have a fellow drinker for company.*"

RISING SUN

MAKES: 2

ice cubes
4 measures vodka
4 teaspoons passion
  fruit syrup

6 measures grapefruit
  juice
ruby grapefruit slices,
  to decorate

*Half-fill a cocktail shaker with ice cubes
and put 6–8 ice cubes into each of 2 old-
fashioned glasses. Add all the remaining
ingredients to the shaker and shake until
a frost forms on the outside or you drop with
exhaustion (should this happen, you are clearly
unfit for joining International Rescue). Strain
the mix over the ice in the glasses, decorate
with a ruby grapefruit slice and serve.*

HAIR RAISER

"Absolutely nothing would make my hair stand on end. I can think of few things less attractive. Tin-Tin loves this drink, however, and says that it reminds her of her first mission, in Thunderbird 3, when Alan's hair stood on end during the sun-probe mission. She's such a darling."

MAKES: 2

cracked ice cubes
2 measures vodka
2 measures sweet
   vermouth

2 measures tonic water
lemon and lime rind
   spirals, to decorate

Put 2–4 cracked ice cubes into 2 highball glasses and pour over the vodka, vermouth and tonic water. Stir lightly, decorate with the lemon and lime rind spirals and serve with straws, unless you find this rather childish – in which case, omit and aim for nonchalant sophistication.

SURF RIDER

SURF RIDER

MAKES: 1

4–5 ice cubes
3 measures vodka
1 measure sweet
  vermouth

juice of ½ lemon
juice of 1 orange
½ teaspoon grenadine

Put the ice cubes into a cocktail shaker. Pour the vodka, vermouth, fruit juices and grenadine over the ice. Shake until a frost forms. Strain and pour into a sour glass. Down the hatch!

"I was once obliged to drive FAB 1 myself, into the open sea off Monte Bianco, making good use of the hydrofoils. I clearly remember a nearby yachtsman remarking: 'I've heard of pink elephants, but a pink Rolls-Royce out at sea? Ridiculous.'"

RUM CRUSTA-CREIGHTON-WARD

MAKES: 1

lime wedge
caster or icing sugar
crushed ice
ice cubes
2 measures dark rum
1 measure Cointreau

2 teaspoons
    maraschino liqueur
2 teaspoons fresh lime
    juice
grapes on cocktail stick,
    to decorate

Moisten the rim of a rocks glass with the lime
wedge and dip about 1 cm (½ in) of the rim
of the glass into the sugar. Fill the glass with
crushed ice and half-fill a cocktail shaker with
ice cubes. Add all the remaining ingredients
to the shaker and shake until a frost forms on
the outside of the shaker. Strain into the glass.
Decorate with grapes à la mode.

*"When we are at home in the
Creighton-Ward mansion, Parker
likes to make this using a glass that
is frosty with cold from the freezer,
then dipped into icing sugar. He says
it reminds him of Christmas in
'an old London pub, M'Lady'."
Each to their own.*

"*I must declare that this is another Parker favourite, making him dwell on the many times he seems to have watched cowboy films as a child. I think there is perhaps a little of the Wild West in all of us — but then danger is practically my middle name.*"

EL DORADO

EL DORADO

MAKES: I

4–5 ice cubes
I measure white rum
I measure advocaat
I measure white crème
   de cacao

2 teaspoons grated
   coconut, plus extra
   to decorate

Put the ice cubes into a cocktail shaker. Add all the remaining ingredients and shake until a frost forms on the outside of the shaker. Strain into a chilled martini glass, decorate with a sprinkling of grated coconut and serve. Parker tends to do this with an accompanying American accent, which can be somewhat grating. You have been warned.

CHAMPAGNE A LA PENELOPE

"After Alan, Tin-Tin and I thwarted a plot against us by those feckless fraudsters on Skyship One, we had champagne but sadly lacked the goodies for this little favourite. Lesser mortals know it by the name of Aria Classic."

MAKES: 1

1 brown sugar cube
3 dashes Angostura bitters
1 measure Grand Marnier

champagne, to top up
orange rind twist, to decorate

Drop the sugar cube into a chilled champagne flute and shake the Angostura bitters over it. Add the Grand Marnier and stir briefly. Top up with champagne, decorate with an orange rind twist and knock back with gusto.

CHABLIS CUP

"This is sure to liven things up at a gathering, even in the company of the dullest of dullards. But for goodness sake watch out for the possibility of 'cocktail cherry choke', which is terribly unsightly and has been known to utterly ruin the most promising of friendships."

MAKES: 15–20

3 ripe peaches, skinned, stoned and sliced
1 orange, thinly sliced
cocktail cherries

3 teaspoons caster sugar
1 bottle Chablis
4 measures Grand Marnier
4 measures Kirsch

Put the fruit and sugar in a punch bowl. Pour in the Chablis, Grand Marnier and Kirsch, and stir. Cover and chill for 1 hour, then get ready to greet your guests with perfect aplomb.

"I remember the poor Tracy boys trying to prevent a tidal wave on the one occasion that Jeff left Scott in charge and came to my farm in Bonga Bonga. I gave him one of these to help him sleep, but it kept the poor man up all night. You have been warned!"

TIDAL WAVE

MAKES: 1

6 ice cubes
1 measure Mandarine
   Napoléon
4 measures bitter
   lemon

1 dash fresh lemon
   juice
lemon slice, to
   decorate

Put the ice cubes into a highball glass. Add the Mandarine Napoléon, bitter lemon and lemon juice and stir well. Decorate with a lemon slice and prepare to dance the night away.

"On very hot summer days, there is simply nothing like Parker's limeade to refresh the spirit. I like to keep a jug of it by the net while hosting tennis parties too, for guests showing indelicate signs of wear."

PARKER'S LIMEADE

PARKER'S LIMEADE

MAKES: 8

6 limes
125 g (4 oz) caster
   sugar
750 ml (1¼ pints)
   boiling water

pinch of salt
ice cubes
mint leaves and lime
   wedges,
   to decorate

I must confess to having never made this myself, but Parker swears that this is the only way to make a decent limeade.

Halve the limes, then squeeze the juice into a large jug. Place the squeezed lime halves into a heatproof jug with the sugar and boiling water and leave to infuse for 15 minutes. Add the salt, stir well, then strain into the jug with the lime juice. Add 6 ice cubes, cover and refrigerate until chilled. To serve, put 3–4 ice cubes in each glass and pour the limeade over them. Decorate with mint leaves and lime wedges.

TENDERBERRY

"This is the yummiest summer drink, and I always offer it to girlfriends when they call round on summer evenings. It makes one think of Wimbledon tennis, blissful picnics and racing at Ascot. Heaven in a glass."

MAKES: I

crushed ice
6–8 strawberries, hulled
I measure grenadine
I measure double cream

I measure dry ginger ale
ground ginger
strawberry, to decorate

Put some crushed ice with the strawberries, grenadine and cream into a blender or food processor and blend for 30 seconds. Pour into a glass. Add the dry ginger ale and stir. Sprinkle a little ground ginger on top and decorate with a strawberry. I sometimes make two – just for myself.

POST-MISSION SHORTS

The dastardly plots of desperate men are easily foiled, but sometimes a quick, short sip of something strong and delicious is just what you need after a mission debrief. These little numbers really hit the spot.

TIN-TIN'S COCKTAIL

TIN-TIN'S COCKTAIL

"Tin-Tin is the most fabulous pilot, especially in a two-seater biplane. She delights in terrifying people by looping the loop – and once flew so low to the mansion rooftop that Parker literally ducked in fright. He promised to rename the Laila Cocktail in her honour if she swore never to tell anyone. Oops!"

MAKES: 1

2 lime wedges
2 strawberries
4 blueberries, plus extra
   to decorate

1 dash mango purée
1 measure raspberry vodka
ice cubes

Muddle the lime wedges, berries, and mango purée in the bottom of a cocktail shaker. Add the vodka and some ice cubes and shake vigorously. Strain it twice, then pour the mix into a chilled martini glass and decorate with 3 extra blueberries on a toothpick. Down in one, if feeling especially overwrought!

STRAWBERRY COSMOPOLITAN

MAKES: 4
50 g (2 oz) caster sugar
200 g (7 oz) hulled and
    quartered strawberries
1 measure vodka
1 measure Cointreau
4 measures soda water
5 measures water

This is relatively demanding, so ask someone else to place the sugar and water in a small saucepan, heat gently until the sugar dissolves, then bring to a boil before removing from the heat. Prompt them to add the strawberries to the pan and squash them into the syrup using the back of a fork, allowing some texture to remain. Politely request that they pour in the remaining ingredients and then tip the entire mixture into an ice-cube tray. After freezing it for 2 hours or until almost solid, you can finally drink the thing, after popping it in a blender for a few quick blasts.

"Is it the sugar or the alcohol that makes this little sipper such a perfect pick-me-up? We always make this for four, even when only Parker and I are at home. I do wonder sometimes if the old safe-cracker spoils me."

TURF, M'LADY?

MAKES: 2

crushed ice
2 measures gin
2 measures dry
   vermouth
2 teaspoons fresh
   lemon juice

2 teaspoons Pernod
lemon slice, to
   decorate

Put some crushed ice into a cocktail shaker and pour over the gin, vermouth, lemon juice, and Pernod. Shake well, then strain into 2 glasses containing more ice. Decorate each glass with a lemon slice and straw. If driving or being driven exceptionally fast, it is perfectly acceptable to overlook the decoration.

"Whenever I go racing I like to drink this cocktail, so Parker has taken to offering it to me after any mission that requires fast driving. Occasionally even while he is driving. Really, that man has an impishness rarely met (though nicely kept in check these days)."

CUCUMBER KYRANO

MAKES: 2

ice cubes

5 measures cucumber-
  infused sake

3 measures gin

1 measure Curaçao

cucumber slices, to
  decorate

Put some ice cubes in a mixing glass with the
sake, gin and Curaçao then stir until thoroughly
chilled. Strain into 2 chilled martini glasses,
decorate with cucumber slices and serve.

Somebody once cheekily suggested this was
really called a Cucumber Sake-tin. I ask you.

Kyrano, who is an expert cocktail-maker, also
told me about a vodka version. Simply pour
5 measures of sake into a mixing glass along
with 2 measures of vodka and 1 measure of
orange Curaçao. Mix, pour, drink. Salut!

"Tin-Tin's father Kyrano showed me this wonderful sake cocktail. If, like me, you find a little excitement very welcome now and again, you will doubtless enjoy the little shock that this drink produces. But don't hesitate – Kyrano assures me that speed is of the essence."

GIN TROPICAL

GIN TROPICAL

MAKES: 1

8 ice cubes
2 measures gin
1 measure fresh lemon juice
1 measure passion fruit juice

½ measure fresh orange juice
soda water, to top up
orange spiral, to decorate

Put 4 of the ice cubes into a cocktail shaker, pour in the gin, lemon juice, passion fruit juice, and orange juice and shake well. Put 4 fresh ice cubes into an old-fashioned glass and strain the cocktail over the ice. Top up with soda water and stir gently. Decorate with an orange spiral. Attempt not to think of tropical Tracy Island and those dashing young men.

"This is the tipple that we at International Rescue drink when we are thinking fondly of Tracy Island after a mission in Europe. I do love London – and Paris, Milan and New York, obviously – but the tropics tend to tug at one's heart. Or perhaps it is merely the gin making one foolishly nostalgic?"

BOURBON PEACH SMASH

"At International Rescue, smashing the plans of ne'er-do-wells is de rigueur, as my governess Miss Pemberton would say. I rather think she would approve of this cocktail, which marvellously dallies with both leaves and fruit."

MAKES: 2

handful of mint leaves
3 peach slices
6 lemon slices
4 teaspoons caster
   sugar

4 measures bourbon
ice cubes
mint sprigs and lemon
   slices, to decorate

Muddle the mint leaves, peach and lemon slices, and sugar in a cocktail shaker. Add the bourbon and some ice cubes and shake well. Pour over fresh ice into 2 old-fashioned glasses. Decorate with a mint sprig and a lemon slice (or even lemon twists, should you feel extravagant).

SWEET AND CHILLI

"When Sir Jeremy Hodge and I were locked in a basement by that nasty piece of work, Dr Godber, I found myself strangely longing for a blast of this cocktail. I felt the chilli would be most effective against the effects of deadly gas. So if in mortal danger, or recovering from some such, you might like to try this little delight."

MAKES: 2

3 measures Scotch whisky
1½ measures fresh
   blood-orange juice
1½ measures Antica Formula
   or sweet vermouth

2 teaspoons agave syrup
ice cubes
red chillies, to decorate

Add the whisky, blood-orange juice, Antica Formula or vermouth, and agave syrup to a cocktail shaker with some ice cubes and shake well until a frost forms on the outside of the shaker. Strain into 2 frozen coupette glasses, decorated with one chilli each. Should your coupettes be frustratingly in one of your other houses, fret not – a martini glass will just as easily fit the bill.

SILK STOCKING

SILK STOCKING

MAKES: 2

drinking chocolate powder
1 ½ measures tequila
1 ½ measures white crème de
    cacao

7 measures single cream
4 teaspoons grenadine
ice cubes

Dampen the rim of 2 chilled martini glasses and dip them into the drinking chocolate powder.

Pour the tequila, crème de cacao, cream and grenadine into a cocktail shaker and add 8–10 ice cubes. Shake vigorously for 10 seconds, then strain into the chilled martini glasses.

"My mother Amelia swore by silk stockings, and her legs were the toast of the town. So I drink this in her honour sometimes, post-mission, because I know how the tales of my exploits would make her laugh. Daddy, of course, would merely roll his eyes skyward and bellow for a gin and tonic."

PARKER'S FRUIT CRUSH

"Parker seems strangely adroit at crushing fruit after putting FAB 1 through its paces, and I must admit to being only too happy to drink the results. I like to sit close to the drinks tray, however, so that a little rum occasionally finds its way into the glass."

MAKES: 2–3

crushed ice
1 ripe peach, skinned, stoned and chopped
1 ripe pear, peeled, cored and chopped
125 g (4 oz) raspberries
7 measures peach juice
pear slices, to decorate

Put some crushed ice with the peach, pear, raspberries and peach juice into a blender or food processor and blend until smooth. Serve in cocktail glasses and decorate with pear slices. When adding a soupçon of secretive rum, remember not to say, "We're in luck, Parker!" through sheer force of habit.

INDEX

ACKNOWLEDGMENTS

Author Acknowledgments

The author would like to acknowledge the indomitable patience of all those close to her, especially her dashing husband, David, and her intrepid daughters, Freya and Lottie. They are exactly the team one would send for in a crisis. She would also like to thank the inspirational Ms Killick, who only drinks cocktails in the finest of places and introduced the author to the delights of a caipirinha. It has been downhill ever since.

Picture Credits

Backgrounds used throughout:
Fotolia GiorgioAtmo; lyricsai; magnia; orangeberry; Svetlana Romanova; Tiax; turbo1019.

Editorial Director: Trevor Davies
Production Controller: Sarah-Jayne Johnson

Produced for Octopus Publishing Group Ltd by Tracy Killick Art Direction and Design and www.editorsonline.org
Art Director: Tracy Killick
Editor: Alice Bowden
Indexer: Hilary Bird